The Trickster Gods and Their Influence on the
Development of Human Culture

Submitted in partial fulfillment of the
requirements for the degree of Bachelor of Arts
at Union Institute & University

Jeffrey Lang
March 23rd, 2015
Professor: Peaco Todd

Abstract

The purpose of this document is an attempt to apprehend in some fashion the meaning, historically, culturally, and psychologically, of the so-called "trickster gods" of our collective mythologies. I have examined here four distinct mythologies to illustrate the commonalities of the trickster archetype existent in all of these diverse cultures. This approach was taken to serve as a springboard from which to launch a case for the relevance of the trickster as a necessary element of man's understanding of himself, and by extension, of the universe.

A note should be made on the use of two words throughout this document: universe and archetype. First, the word universe is not to be understood in the standard cosmological sense; rather it is a word defining the Objective Universe, which is the sum total of everything that makes up our shared external reality. This Objective Universe includes not only the material universe that we apprehend with our five senses, but also the natural laws (attributed to the governance of gods, or the neteru, within this document) that govern the interaction of all of the elements of this material universe. Second, archetype is used in the Jungian sense of a psychological presence of a fundamental reality, or what Plato would refer to as the "first forms." These archetypes exist as the underlying metaphysical and/or psychological mechanisms that are given voice and vision by the individual as well as mythologies of man. It is important to note that mythology does not necessarily mean the relics of an ancient religion in this sense, but rather any established imagery that conveys an internally consistent narrative as well as a set of qualitative values for the elements within the narrative. In this way, the "Star Wars" movies are equally as valid a mythology as the Classical Greek mythology. The essence of the mythology is simply presence of some sort of manifestation of recognizable archetypes, and an internal consistency within the narrative.

    One final note: the trickster seems to break the rule of maintaining an internal consistency in each mythology, but that behavior *is* the essence of the trickster. The trickster's place outside of the laws of predictability is his expression of internal consistency within each mythology.

    This work will follow the following structure:

Chapter 1: A brief introduction to Norse mythology and the meaning of Loki as the trickster.

Chapter 2: The role of Prometheus's manifestation of the trickster archetype in man's progress through opposition to natural law.

Chapter 3: An attempt to understand the necessity for action and change in the natural world as illustrated by the Aztec trickster god Tezcatlipoca.

Chapter 4: The incorporation of all of these elements in man's peculiar place as an unnatural being in the natural world, expressed through the Egyptian god Set.

Table of Contents

Preface
5

Chapter 1: Loki, and the Imperative of Progress
13

Chapter 2: The Promethean Ideal of Adversarial Man
39

Chapter 3: Tezcatlipoca and the Immediacy of Action
59

Chapter 4: Set and the Egyptian Model of Balance
83

References
104

Preface

I consider my first college experience, at the University of Cincinnati, to be my necessary miserable failure in the learning process. Between the year of my graduation, 1998, and my return to college in 2014, I pursued my own personal interests while unintentionally building a career as a chef. After a business-destroying flood, the death of a few close friends, and a particularly memorable personal meltdown, I made the decision to cease my previously amicable relationship with alcohol. At that point, I knew that I had to do something new with my life to make up for years of spinning my wheels, but I still had not had the cartoon light bulb appear over my head. During an extremely brief stay at what I thought would be my dream job, everything "clicked" for me.

    I knew that my interests, psychology, religion, philosophy, literature, mythology and folklore, would not likely be a key part of my life in food and beverage co-packaging. I immediately knew that I had to go back to school, and this time I knew why I was going to school: to learn. I wasn't going to college because it was what was expected of me, and I wasn't going to college to increase my marketability. In fact, I think that I may be one of the least marketable persons that I have ever encountered. But regardless, I needed to go back to college to formally explore the subjects that I had been pursuing on my own time.

In my first term, I studied the role of the individual consciousness in both initiatory and authoritarian religions. During this study, I had three very significant academic developments. First, I had to learn to put aside my own beliefs about religion and examine the systems objectively. Second, I formally did the research to "connect the dots" between religion, philosophy, psychology, and a critical view of some of the "whys" of the shaping of modern culture. The third and final piece I took away from my first study was a confirmation of my suspicion that there are numerous unseen connections beneath the surface of the way things appear.

This was the beginning of one of the two guiding philosophies that now direct my academic, professional, and personal pursuits. This first new philosophy pertains to the dire, and I do not think that dire is too strong an adjective here, need for an all-encompassing approach to understand the why and wherefore of life on Earth. The fields of philosophy, psychology, archaeology, physics, art history, etc., need to be viewed as interconnected and integral pieces of our past, and more importantly, our future.

This led to my next independent study, an investigation into the Jungian archetypal imagery at work in the writing of H.P. Lovecraft. In this study, I framed Lovecraft's fiction, as well as the esoteric arts that influenced him, within the context of a psychological analysis of his understanding of the world. This study was extremely successful for me, in that I began to examine *everything* around me to see how each piece interacts with the whole to create my own subjective universe. What I found in Lovecraft's writing was a belief in the absolute impersonality of the universe. His stories illustrated an almost crippling insecurity with what he perceived as the malevolence within the chaos of the universe. This led to my other guiding philosophy, and to my culminating study.

My second philosophy concerns the improbable vector of the human race arising out of the chaos of the universe. Our ancestors personified that which they did not understand in their gods. But out of these gods, one archetypal figure is wholly unnatural and alien to the natural world, the trickster god. The trickster god represents that "X Factor" that makes humans wholly different from the rest of the living world. The presence of a conscious mind, capable of self-examination and reflection, gives man the unique ability to perceive the unseen world around us, and to interpret the relationships between actions and reactions. This conscious mind also imparts man with that most divine attribute—the ability to create that which has never existed before. The trickster god embodies this "door" between the primal chaos of the unformed universe and the objective universe that we are all bound to by our five senses. The trickster is the universe's creative consultant to the living art of creation.

It is in this spirit that I have chosen to study the mythologies of ancient Egypt, Greece, Northern Europe, and the Aztec world, to try to understand why these gods were necessary to our ancestors. I intend to see how the direction of these cultures was shaped during periods when these gods were honored and worshipped. I intend to try to see the world through the eyes of these cultures, momentarily, and understand the trickster on his own terms. My ultimate goal is to pluck from the darkness of the past a few more connections between religion and the psyche of man, and hopefully, to apply this knowledge in my life. Philosophy, after all, is meaningless if it exists merely in theory. It is in the application of these philosophies that we carry forth the torch of our ancestors. It is in the application of these philosophies that we create the world as we wish to see it.

Chapter 1
Loki, and the Imperative of Progress

The Germanic peoples, particularly the Northern Germanic peoples, existed in near isolation for a particularly lengthy period before the inevitable Christianization of Europe. Due to their geographic isolation, the Norse avoided the cultural dilutions that many other Indo-European peoples experienced through war and conquests. This peculiar position resulted in a wholly unique refinement of the Northern Heathen beliefs. The Neolithic paganism of Northern Europe slowly transformed into the Heathen religion that we now know through Norse Mythology.

To understand the world of the Norse peoples, we must first understand their unique cosmology. Unlike the vast majority of mythologies, the Norse universe, or more appropriately multiverse, is a cyclical system of creation, destruction, and rebirth. As opposed to a belief that one side—good or evil—will ultimately win out, rather all of creation will consume itself to accommodate the next rebirth. But the natural laws of the universe, represented by the Norse gods, the Æsir, lead to a stasis in the created world. There must be an agent of change to introduce the conflict required to allow this cycle to continue. This agent of change is embodied in Loki. Loki is a quintessential example of the archetypal trickster god. His actions, though initially perceived as mischievous or even wicked, bring to the universe the changes that allow life itself to exist. If the Æsir are the principles of natural law, Loki is the black spark that prompts them into action. Loki is the chaotic seed of the acausal universe that defines the dynamic change of life.

This leads to the inevitable question: "Where did the multiverse come from?" The foundational source of Norse mythology is a collection of Old Norse poems, known collectively as the "Poetic Edda." In his new translation, <u>The Elder Edda: A Book of Viking Lore</u>, editor Andy Orchard (2011) arranges the poems in a chronological sequence, beginning with *Völuspá:* The prophecy of the seeress, a poetic synopsis of the creation of the universe, and the first full cycle of destruction and rebirth. The first two stanzas, at first glance seem to be merely illustrative to set up the narrative, but upon closer inspection, they reveal a deeper insight to the Heathen understanding of the universe.

> A hearing I ask of all
> holy offspring,

> the higher and lower
> of Heimdall's brood.
> Do you want me,
> Corpse-father, to
> tally up well,
> ancient tales of folk,
> from the first I
> recall?
>
> I recall those giants,
> born early on,
> who long ago
> brought me up;
> nine worlds I recall,
> nine wood-dwelling
> witches,
> the famed tree of
> fate down under the
> earth (p. 5).

The first thing to note is the implication that the world of physical existence extends far beyond the dawn of Odin, here referred to as Corpse-father. To understand what this means about the nature of the pantheon of the Norse gods, the significance of the giants of the age before the dawn of Odin is extremely significant.

In his collection <u>The Vikings – Philosophy and History – From Ragnar LodBrok to Norse Mythology</u>, George Mentz (2014) summarizes the primary and most simplistic relationship between the Æsir and the giants: "The chaotic world-mass is produced by the blending of heat and cold, and this chaos quickens into the form of the giant Ymer. The Asas arc the beneficent forces and elements in nature. They separate from the evil and destructive elements (the giants), conquer them by their divine power, and create from them the world" (p. 24). This is the fundamental basis for the need of the trickster, Loki. The Æsir have separated themselves from the giants, or Thurses, but are *of* the giants, and as such, their powers as divine principles are inextricably tied to the Thurses. They must have a living link between themselves and the primal chaos from whence they originate. Loki is this link. Loki is himself a Thurse, of the frost giants, yet Odin makes him a blood brother to him. This is the most fundamental truth of the trickster—he is not simply a mischief-maker for his own amusement, he is the link between the formless chaos of creation and the forces that bring forth order.

Of all of the material in the Poetic Edda concerning Loki, the most significant can be found in the poem *Lokasenna*: Loki's home truths. This poem begins with Loki being banished from a feast held by the god Ægir for slaying Ægir's son Fimafeng out of jealousy. When Loki defiantly walks back into the feast, he is shunned, and converses with the gods:

> *Loki said*:
> 'Do you recall, Odin,
> when long ago

we two blended
together our blood:
you said you would
never partake of ale
unless it was
brought to us both.'

Odin said:
'Up then, Vidar, and
let the wolf's father
take up a seat at the
feast,
lest Loki speaks of
us with reproach
inside Ægir's halls'
(Orchard, 2011, p.
84-85).

If we see Odin, the All-father, as the first principle of man's consciousness, then his relationship here to Loki says something profound and often un-acknowledged about the nature of man. This slaying of Ægir's son seems to be a vicious and malevolent act, but every action must be viewed in the perspective of the eternal cycle of destruction and rebirth to be understood for what it is. The ideas of right and wrong lose their arbitrary meanings and are replaced by progress or stagnation. The question arises however, why would the Norse poets feel compelled to have their trickster Loki murder the son of a god? The most obvious answer is that this act, and Odin's reaction to it, proves beyond a shadow of a doubt that Odin cannot exist without his blood brother Loki. Order cannot exist without chaos.

It is out of necessity that we must look again to Odin to understand the nature of Loki. Just as Loki represents that gate to the ultimate chaos, Odin represents the principle of isolate intelligence through which we apprehend Loki. One of the greatest accomplishments of Odin was his receiving of the gift of the runes, which he then gave to man. It should be first noted where the word "rune" originates. Rune comes from the Norse word "runa." Runa is the Norse word for the mysteries of the universe. It is akin to the Greek "mysterion," which represents the mystical meeting-place of man and the divine. Odin subjected himself to a great ordeal in his quest for the runes, which is told in the poem *Havamal* in the Poetic Edda.

> I know that I hung
> on that windy tree,
> spear-wounded,
> nine full nights,
> given to Odin, myself
> to myself,
> on that tree rose
> from roots
> that no man ever
> knows.
>
> They gave me
> neither bread nor
> drink from horn,
> I peered down
> below.
> I clutched the runes,
> screaming I grabbed
> them,

and then sank back (Orchard, 2011, p. 35).

There are several vitally important details here that provide insight to the Northern heathen's ordering of the world. The first detail is that Odin hung from the tree, Yggdrasil, the tree of life, peering *down*. Peering down below the tree's roots would put Odin's gaze fixed on the uncreated frozen chaos, the source of Loki and the frost giants. The gift of the runes, both written communication and the archetypal secret of creation, comes from this same chaos that brings the world the trickster. The second important detail in this tale is Odin's sacrifice of himself to himself. He tells us that you cannot make offerings to the force of chaos; rather, the chaos demands you undergo this ordeal for the benefit of yourself.

Now, before we move away from the runes, we need to look at one rune in particular. As each rune has both a phonetic value as well as a mystical value, Thurisaz, which later became the Old English *thorn*, or *th* sound, represents the violent force of chaos and the Thurses. In his book <u>ALU: An Advanced Guide to Operative Runology</u>, Edred Thorsson (2012) discusses the fundamental teaching of Thurisaz. "The Æsir are seen to evolve up from the Thursar. This curiously makes the Thursar both inferior to the Æsir—because the Æsir represent a superior form of later development—and superior to the Æsir in that they are more basic and hence ultimately outlive the Æsir" (p. 54). Now this first reinforces the necessary relationship between the Æsir and the Thurses, but it also places Loki in an altogether different classification from every other being in existence. Loki is of the frost giants, but he is not a frost giant. He lives in Asgard with the Æsir, and as a blood brother to Odin, but he is not one of the Æsir. Loki is the perpetual outsider in all of creation. Every mythology and religion has this archetypal trickster, one who is wholly alien to both man and the gods, but in the Norse mythology, Loki is in the company of the gods. Again we see attention to progress and the perpetuation of the cycle of death and rebirth rather than a focus on the arbitrary labels of good and evil.

The incident that ultimately turned the Æsir against Loki was the slaying of Odin's son Baldr through trickery. Baldr was the favorite son of Odin and Frigg, and he was praised among the gods because of his brilliant shining countenance. Frigg loved Baldr so much that she forced every plant and animal in the nine worlds to swear an oath not to harm Baldr. In doing this, she did not ask for an oath from the mistletoe, because it was such a small and harmless plant that it could never harm Baldr. Loki, upon learning of this through trickery, fashioned a dart from the mistletoe stalk. In Asgard, the gods were feasting and making a game of throwing their weapons at Baldr, knowing that their weapons could not touch him. Loki asked Baldr's blind brother Höd if he would like Loki to help him throw a dart to participate in the game. The Poetic Edda tells the story thusly:

> I saw for Baldr, the
> blood-stained god,
> Odin's son, his fate
> fully settled;

> there stood
> blooming, above the ground,
> meagre, mighty
> beautiful: mistletoe.
>
> From that plant, that
> seemed so slender,
> Höd learned to shoot
> a dangerous dart of harm;
> Baldr's brother was
> quickly born:
> that son of Odin
> learned to kill one
> night old (Orchard, 2011, p. 9-10).

This event, within the context of the story of the gods, was necessary to set things in motion for the final conflict of the gods, Ragnarök. His deed was deemed so unforgivable by the Æsir, that he was hunted down and punished in an extremely brutal manner. But, we must understand why the poets who wrote this felt the need to include it in their narrative.

The customs of the northern Heathens were often a reverence to the natural phenomena, which they personified as their gods. In the case of Loki the trickster, these customs were more complex. Loki, being a non-natural outsider god, required non-natural worship. The Norse Men replayed the story of Loki causing the slaying of Baldr in ritual. As Lewis Hyde (2010) explains in <u>Trickster Makes This World: Mischief, Myth, and Art</u>, "To see how this might be, consider that in ancient times the deadly weapon Loki discovers, the mistletoe, was used ritually in a manner suggesting that the drama of Loki and Baldr once mirrored the solar or agricultural calendar" (p. 103). The purpose of this ritual was not to honor the gods, but rather, it was a magical working to try to bring about change in the natural world, just as Loki's chaotic spark brought about change to the natural law of the Æsir. With the brilliance of Baldr's countenance being a metaphor for the golden sun, Hyde explains the mistletoe ritual: "It was the custom in northern countries to gather mistletoe at Midsummer's Eve, that is to say, at the summer solstice, the point in time when the sun reverses its course and spends the rest of the year dropping lower toward the horizon. In ritual, then, picking the mistletoe 'causes' the sun's decline, just as, in myth, Loki's discovery of that green weapon causes the death of Baldr the Bright" (p. 103). This is a peculiarly Northern ritual, as their geographical location causes, from their perspective, the sun to "disappear" from their sky for long periods in the winter.

While on the subject of magic, it is important to look at another of Loki's most important acts—the crafting of the weapons of the gods. Another of Loki's acts that at first seems like mischief at best, and malice at worst, is again, the correction of course to allow the final battle of Ragnarök to play out as prophesied. The poems of the Poetic Edda were reworked into a more cohesive narrative, fleshed out with details from various oral traditions by an Icelandic politician named Snorri Sturluson. In her book about the life of Sturluson, <u>Song of the Vikings</u>, Nancy Marie Brown (2012) tells this story of Loki's transgression and reparation: "Another time Loki, out of mischief, cut off the goddess Sif's long, golden hair. Her husband, the mighty Thor, was not amused" (p. 120). This flagrant attack on the honor of Sif, and more importantly, the ability of her husband Thor to defend her honor, was met by a threat of a violent beating for Loki. But Loki, always using non-natural means to grease the wheels of progress, proposes a solution: he will have the dwarven craftsmen fashion for Sif a wig of brilliant gold that will grow just as her real hair. Loki comes back with the wig, and also five other treasures that feature prominently in the fate of the nine worlds.

Brown explains that Loki has had the dwarves fashion for Freyr a "magic ship 'which had a fair wind as soon as its sail was hoisted'…Another was Odin's spear which 'Never stopped in its thrust'…the gold ring that, every ninth night, spawned eight more rings like itself…a boar with bristles of gold that could run across the sky faster than a horse" (p. 120). The final gift that Loki brought from the dwarves was for Thor, and it was his mighty hammer mjolnir.

This weapon is what Thor uses to defeat Loki's son, the Midgard Serpent, in the final battle of Ragnarök. What is also remarkable about this is how Loki once again uses his cunning to get these gifts from the dwarves. He offers the Dwarves his head in exchange for the treasures. Loki informs the dwarf who is to collect his debt "the head was his, but not the neck" (p. 120). This is the nature of the trickster. The natural world is bound by the causal laws enforced by the first principles, or gods, but Loki is a personified metaphysical shortcut. His methods are wholly unnatural, yet they do not break the natural laws that govern the universe.

To bring us to the final conflict of Ragnarök, we must first return to Loki's exploits in the *Lokasenna*. In his work <u>The Trial of Loki: A Study in Nordic Heathen Morality</u>, Alan James

(2013) examines the motivations of Loki and the Æsir in Loki's provocations in Ægir's banquet hall. Loki's exchanged accusations with the other gods are of a particularly potent nature in heathen times—they are accusations of homosexuality and sexual immorality. This particular characterization, known as "nid," as James explains "...was not something to be taken lightly. In 12th and 13th century Iceland nid was a killing matter" (p. 8). For Loki to unleash this barrage of insults on the Æsir, the other gods could have justifiably killed him. So what reason would the Æsir have to allow this transgression to go unchecked? "They allow him to establish his hostility, and while giving him the fairest possible hearing they manoeuvre him into boasting of his guilt" (p. 10). This gives the Æsir the justification they need to bind Loki so that he can do no more harm.

Loki, in punishment for all of the exploits that he boasted of in the banquet hall is subjected to a series of acts of extraordinary cruelty. The gods turn one of Loki's sons into a wolf and compel him to kill his brother. The entrails of Loki's slain son are then used to bind him to a stone. Above his head, a poisonous serpent is hung by the goddess Skadi. When Loki finally escapes his bonds, he and his kin, the giants avenge his torment. The Poetic Edda, again in *Völuspá,* the opening gambit of Ragnarök is described

> The standing ash of
> Yggdrasil shudders,
> the aged tree groans,
> and the giant breaks free.
> All are afraid on the
> paths of Hel,

> before Surt's kin
> swallows it up
> (Orchard, 2011, p. 12).

This is the beginning of the prophesied final conflict, in which the Æsir, led by Odin, and the giants, led by Loki, must destroy each other.

A note should be made about the word Ragnarök itself. The word has been mistranslated for so long that its wrong meaning has come into accepted use. Lewis Hyde (2010) explains the root of the word: "In Icelandic, the gods are called reginn, which means 'organizing powers.' Ragna- is the possessive plural of this word. The suffix –rök means 'marvels, fate, doom.' Ragnarök thus means 'the gods' wonders' or 'the gods' fate/doom' (p. 102). The popular phrase "twilight of the gods" comes about because "...the second half of the word has become confused with røkkr, 'twilight,' and it is often translated as such, as into Wagner's German: Götterdämmerung..." (p. 102). This mistranslation leads to an imprecise understanding of Ragnarök. "Twilight," being the time of day before sunrise or after sunset, gives the impression that this is a waning or dark time when the gods fall from power. The true meaning of the word, "fate/doom of the gods," is more accurate. This is the fate of the gods, it has been foretold, and therefore, predestined. Loki has thrown wide the doors of chaos to bring back balance to the universe.

The trickster, symbolized for the Norse as Loki, is that necessary spark of chaos that keeps the universe progressing. All of the other gods represent natural law, and an unchanging mandate to remain constant. When these forces of nature are unchallenged, whether in the universe, or in the microcosm that we call man, growth ceases; change ceases; and life loses meaning. In the most extreme terms, we have seen this in Hitler's Germany. The unfaltering devotion to the "Fatherland" was a cultural remnant of the archetype of the All-father Odin. This society was necessarily doomed, because the chaotic seed of change and creation was cut out. The only egress available for change was in the form of Allied troops and their armaments.

This aspect of the self, the trickster, is always at work in the psyche of man. Loki lives in the happy accidents of discovery. He lives in that most human ability—the ability to ask "Why?" This confrontation between the order of conditioned behavior and the chaos of creative change leads to a rebirth. The Völuspá ends with the rebirth of the untouched universe, again

awakening refreshed and renewed:

> All the unsown fields
> will grow,
> all harm will be
> healed, Baldr will
> come;
> Höd and Baldr will
> inhabit Hropt's
> victory-halls,
> sanctuaries of the
> slain-gods: do you
> know yet, or what?
>
> Then there comes
> the dark dragon
> flying,
> the glittering snake
> up from Moon-wane
> hills,
> it bears in its
> wings—and flies
> over the plain—
> dead bodies: Spite-
> striker; now she
> must sink (Orchard,
> 2011, p. 14).

And so too must the unchallenged enemies of our growth sink, once the trickster has forced the door to our unformed self.

Chapter 2
The Promethean Ideal of Adversarial Man

The mythology of ancient Greece stands apart in many ways from the mythologies of other ancient civilizations. Like many other ancient mythologies, it answers some basic questions concerning the nature of the universe and the forces ordering this universe. Also like many other mythologies, it provides a mandate for the way in which life is to be. But the golden angle of diversion inherent to the Greek mythology lies in a second mandate. This is the mandate of action inherent in the gift of fire from Prometheus. This act of rebellion, stealing fire from the heavens, is not only the mark of the trickster, but bestowing this gift unto man inherently changes man's nature to incorporate this trickster into his self.

To understand the significance of fire, introduced to man, we need to look at every aspect of this interaction. First, there is the nature of fire itself, as a divine tool of the gods. This fire, a creation of the gods, is one of the tools that forged the world and all of its wonders. To appreciate the vector of this divine fire-force, we should begin, as it were, at the beginning. The first gods of the Greeks, those who brought the world into order, were the Titans. This is not unlike the Norse lineage of creation wherein the giants, or Thurses, existed as primordial gods before the gods of the Common Era came into being. The twelve original Titans ruled the heavens and the earth for some time before their offspring began influencing the universe. Some of these Titans, such as Cronus, were so unwilling to cede power that they killed, or in the case of Cronus, ate their offspring. This was the first of the three classical ages of Greece. In his overview of this mythology, <u>Greek Mythology: The Complete Guide to Greek Mythology, Ancient Greece, Greek Gods, Zeus, Hercules, Titans and More!</u> Nick Plesiotis (2014) explains the three periods like this:

> The first is the Age of the Gods from the beginning of time and the creation of the world and humankind. The second is the Age of Gods and Mortals when men interacted with deities, also resulting in demigods. The third is the Age of Heroes where the focus is more on the acts of men with some divine intervention (p. 2).

Where fire, man, and Prometheus intersect should be properly called the end of the Age of Gods.

Through trickeries, alliances, and battles in the heavens, a younger generation of gods wrested power away from the Titans and established their rule atop Mount Olympus. The highest of these Olympians was Zeus, who was above all the arbiter of the actions of all gods and men. But among these Olympians, there existed another intermediary class of gods who were born of Titans, but older than the Olympians. Prometheus was of this class, being born of the Titan Iapetus. In this light, a comparison to Loki could be made; Prometheus is of the older, primal powers that ordered themselves from the great Chaos, but sat on Mount Olympus with the younger gods. He is, also like Loki, necessarily an outsider, as his nature is not of those around him.

In this ordering of the universe, we see an unresolvable stasis: the gods dictate the natural laws of the universe, and man is at the mercy of these gods, just like every other creature of the land, air, or sea. In Hesiod's (2014) <u>Works and Days</u>, he dramatizes the conflict between man and the Olympians:

> For the gods keep hidden from men the means of life. Else you would easily do work enough in a day to supply you for a full year even without working; soon you would put away your rudder over the smoke, and the fields worked by ox and sturdy mule would run to waste. But Zeus in his anger of his heart hid it, because Prometheus

> the crafty deceived him; therefore he planned sorrow and mischief against men (p. 3).

In this state, man is powerless in the face of the natural world. He must work in the light and cease working in the dark. He can create nothing; rather he is at the mercy of what springs forth from the earth. In this way, man is essentially a puppet or amusement for Zeus. And let us remember, Zeus is not the Prime. Zeus is simply the current torch-holder of the gods. He is not the uncreated one, yet he holds all others in thrall beneath him.

Prometheus, himself being an outsider, sympathized with man in his imposed state of inferiority. It is his dissent with Zeus that leads him to elevate man to the level of god. It is in the ability to knowingly and with intention conceive of and create that which has never been created that the true power of a god lies. So in order to give man this power, Prometheus devises a plan to steal fire from the heavens and deliver it to man. Zeus, in his anger, punishes not only Prometheus, but man as well. "Son of Iapetus, surpassing all in cunning, you are glad that you have outwitted me and stolen fire—a great plague to you yourself and to men that shall be. But I will give men as the price for fire an evil thing in which they may all be glad of heart while they embrace their own destruction" (p. 3). Surely this metaphor rings true with all of the aspects of fire, both literal and symbolic, as countless ages of man have engineered their own demise.

Before discussing the punishment of Prometheus, it is important to understand the significance of fire. In a purely literal and utilitarian sense, fire gives man the ability to see in the dark, to cook previously inedible foods, to warm him in the cold, and also to harness the destructive powers of fire. On a deeper level, we need to understand why the ancient Greeks felt a need to use fire as the symbol of seizing power from the gods. In Ami Ronnberg's (2010) The Book of Symbols, the significance is explained thusly: "The first sparks of human self-discovery coincided with fire-making and fire-tending. Everywhere, fire was imagined as a deity, part animal, part spirit, living, breathing, eating, propagating; a trickster and shape-shifter whom we engage and propitiate" (p. 82). It is in this symbolic understanding of fire that we understand the transgression of Prometheus. Stealing this power and bringing the knowledge of its use to man is the quintessential destabilizing act of the trickster.

In this light, man, now becoming aware of his creative and destructive capacities, must re-order his conception of his own place within the universe. The gift of Prometheus makes man an unnatural entity, existing as an adversarial foil to Zeus and his Olympian Law. In fact, the self-knowledge inherent in the mastery of fire is an initiation into the Olympian mysteries. It is this duality of the mortal body and the divine consciousness, capable of abstract creation, which makes man unnatural, just as Prometheus' dual nature made him unnatural. To use the common metaphor of fire as enlightenment, man did not know his nature until he was given the gift of Prometheus.

For his part in this theft, Prometheus was punished severely. The Greek Epic Poet Aeschylus (1995) in <u>Prometheus Bound</u> gives to us from the mouth of Prometheus a detail of his punishment:

> Behold in chains confined an ill-starred god,
> The detested of Zeus and rejected of all
> The celestial band that assembleth aloft
> In the heavenly courts of the Highest,
> For my too great love of the children of men!
> Pheu, pheu! What again is the murmur I hear
> As of birds hard by?
> And the air is astir with the whispering beat
> Of their hurrying wings.
> Oh, fearful is all that approacheth (p. 7).

Prometheus' punishment is four-fold: he is cast out from the company of Zeus; he is chained immobile to a great stone; he is presented in his shame for all gods and men to witness and mock; and he is defenseless against the birds of prey that will ceaselessly devour him for eternity. As this is an affair of the gods, the table is slanted in favor of Zeus—Prometheus will heal every night, thus allowing every day to bring a fresh horror of avian-borne disembowelment. The step into initiation can never be retreated upon. Prometheus must bear his torments for the transgression of allowing man to see that Mighty Zeus, the supreme Olympian, was neither infallible nor omnipotent.

To punish man, Zeus devised another devious plan. Christopher Dell (2012), in <u>Mythology: The Complete Guide to our Imagined Worlds</u>, explains, "In the Greek myth of Pandora, this haunting figure—the first woman—was created to punish humanity for Prometheus' theft of fire" (p. 132). It is this symbol of the sacred feminine through which Zeus exposes man to his wrath: "But Pandora was also given a large jar: curious, she opened it, releasing every type of evil into the world. Only hope was left inside" (p. 132). Man, with his newfound gift of fire, must now contend with all of the evils of the world. But why was this punishment personified in the form of a woman?

Gary S. Boroff (2014) in his book <u>Crop Circles, Jung, and the Reemergence of the Archetypal Feminine</u>, raises an interesting point. "The movement of humanity out of enchantment with the natural world and into conscious self-awareness and the intellectual and scientific bloom in the modern era can be seen to be archetypally masculine" (p. 141). Prometheus' act of seizing a part of the powers of the gods for man represents a huge shift in the psyche of a civilization. Man, with his new abilities to master the world around him and conquer with fire, has been deceived into believing in a false dichotomy. The idea that a civilization can either conquer or create, but not both, is the secret of Pandora's jar. There is a condition to man's self-awareness that is not always immediately grasped: when one aspect of man's nature is empowered, all aspects of man's nature are empowered. The destructive nature of the gift of Prometheus is represented by a turning away from the archetypal feminine. With Prometheus shackled to a stone, man is left without a guide to show him how to use this fire. The destabilizing act of taking fire from the heavens must be felt on earth as well. With the trickster bound, the universe will attempt to find stasis once more.

This transition from the Age of the Gods to the Age of Gods and Mortals is a precarious point in the psyche of man. The human consciousness can be quite shocked when the trickster tells us "Everything that the gods can do, you can do too." This transition requires fluidity, or else fractures will occur. Deldon Anne McNeely (1996) explains this in her book <u>Mercury Rising: Women, Evil and the Trickster Gods</u>: "It is said that in times of transition when shapes are shifting, we have to be able to dance. Now we are in transition, and we have a tension between those who would dance, and those who would hold still and hope to keep old forms in place" (p. 109). This perfectly describes what is really being expressed in the myth of Prometheus. If we take the myth as a story of one sequence of events that caused a shift in the arc of human development at one time, then we have one very limited understanding of the message. The myth exists because this struggle between order and chaos is constant in the psyche of the individual.

So often in the mythologies of ancient civilizations, we see time as cyclical, with events happening over and over again. Could this be explained by the fact that our unconscious mind is constantly in conflict with the false and temporary stabilities that our conscious mind tries to create? There is an element of inevitability in so many of these myths, and this is because these myths are our way of apprehending the abstract truths of our minds; our minds that defy all laws of nature and logic and seem to exist in direct opposition to every other force acting upon our sense-based bodies.

David Williams (2013) draws some lines between this trickster archetype and our human consciousness in <u>The Trickster Brain: Neuroscience, Evolution, and Narrative</u>. First, we must look at the natures of Prometheus and Pandora. "Prometheus, whose name means 'forethought,' was wise and able to tell the future and was on the side of human mortals, giving them fire" (p. 214). We see that this trickster aspect of our consciousness, knowing full well the consequences of disturbing the natural order of things, gives us this gift of self-awareness. Williams goes on: "Zeus was irate that Prometheus had given humans fire, and in punishment he had a mortal woman created of unbelievable beauty who would lie and deceive. Pandora" (p.214). Pandora, the ideal of feminine beauty, embodies that aspect of our consciousness that we are trained to be afraid of, but are seduced into opening. The creation of Pandora in response to Prometheus' transgression is a mythological expression of our irresistible urge to touch the fire. The flame of self-awareness is not a lightly given gift, and to revere it in the image of a god is the closest to a proper understanding of our unconscious mind that mankind has grasped thus far.

The ancient Greeks who were initiated into the mysteries of these gods must have grasped this incredible responsibility inherent in holding the fire of self-awareness. Without this insight, would Plato have conceived of his first forms? Certainly The Republic arose out of reverence for this divinity in the consciousness of man. But, we do a great disservice to ourselves as individuals and as a species when we do not acknowledge the source of this flame. Consciousness is taken for granted as something inherent in our "human-ness." How often does anyone ponder the significance that the divine flame of the gods can live within the human mind? The understanding of the three ages of the Greeks disintegrates when man grasps that he is just as capable as Zeus of wielding the sacred fire. The distinction between man and god exists only when man imposes this distinction upon himself.

Aeschylus (1995) gives to us the great noble truth of Prometheus when he explains his actions:

> Easy for him who keeps his foot outside
> The miry clay to give advice to one
> In trouble. All this was known to me:
> I willed to sin, I willed it, I confess.

> My help to man brought suffering to myself (p. 12-13).

The foreknowledge of the outcome does not alter the course of the trickster. Just as Loki gave the magical weapons to the Æsir that would help destroy his kin in the final battle, Prometheus knew that Zeus would punish him fiercely for delivering fire to man. But in both cases, these actions had to be carried out for the universe to move forward. The man-made notions of wrong and right are irrelevant. The trickster does that which must be done, regardless of the consequence. And in the consciousness of each man, artificial limits and taboos must be broken for growth to occur. This initiation requires sacrifice of the self, to the self. And what walks out of the other side of the fire, is a truer form of the self.

Chapter 3
Tezcatlipoca and the Immediacy of Action

The Aztec world, contrary to the assumptions of the conquering Spaniards, was a highly ordered and complex world. The fundamental nature of this ordering of the world was rooted in a complex blending of a fixed determination of the individual's place in the universe, and a knowledge that anything could be changed in an instant at the whim of the god Tezcatlipoca. The Aztec people inherited their basic conception of the world and their religious principles from their predecessors, the Chichimec people of Mexico. The Chichimec were a rootless people, but with the designation of a central capital, coupled with the emergence of a dominant warrior class, the Aztec people emerged. The primary idiosyncrasy of the Aztecs was in their primary supreme deity, Tezcatlipoca. Tezcatlipoca was a trickster god of the strictest sense, and his often-arbitrary dealings with man and god alike were emulated in every aspect of the Aztec world. The Aztecs leave us with two questions: Why did they elevate a trickster to the level of almighty, and how did this peculiar choice dictate the course of the Aztecs?

To begin apprehending the meaning of the Aztec world, we must first understand their mythology. The mythology of the Aztecs, while certainly understood differently depending on where one stood in the social strata, was essentially accepted literally and used as a mandate for the ordering of one's life. Burr Cartwright Brundage (1983) untangles and offers interpretation of the Aztec mythology and its impact on the Aztec people in his book <u>The Fifth Sun: Aztec Gods, Aztec World</u>. He begins his timeline of the Aztec mythology with the actions of a historical, and not a mythological, figure. This is an excellent way to begin comprehending the inseparable nature of life and mythology.

> On a day in the past—perhaps somewhere around the year A.D. 1250—the great Chichimec conqueror Xolotl solemnized his newly won possession of lands in Central Mexico formerly belonging to the Toltecs. He did this by dispatching four arrows from a mountaintop, one toward each of the four directions. A cable of dried grass, coarsely twined, was placed in the shape of a ring on the ground and burned, the ashes being

> scattered also to the
> four winds (p. 3).

This starting point serves to give us a frame of reference for the beginning of the settling of the Chichimec people—defining the beginning of the Aztec people—as well as defining the Aztec territory by the order established by the gods.

The physical orientation of the material world was defined by the gods, in the personification of the rising sun. This heliocentric idea of the gods existing in natural phenomena is a commonality among many ancient mythologies. Brundage explains it like this: "The four directions had been made explicit for him by the sun god himself, who, by first bringing day into the world, once and for all had proclaimed what was to be the correct orientation" (p. 4). What distinguishes the Aztec perception of the physical world was the inclusion of a fifth direction. "The Aztecs considered that the node where the coordinates crossed was itself a direction—in fact it was considered the primary direction" (p. 4). This fifth direction was both the center as well as the inside of the earth itself, and "...this center was held by the most ancient of all the gods, the god of fire, whose name was Xiuhteuctli, Lord of the Year" (p. 5). This fire-god was not a god in the sense of the rest of the Aztec pantheon of gods in that he was not a conscious intervening agent in the world. Instead, he was the primal foundation of creation, as well as the force that defined all of the natural law of the Aztec world.

This "god of the center" is not unlike the Norse Thurses or the Greek Titans, as he was an older, primal force of chaos and disorder that served to provide both the order of the universe as well as the energy of existence itself. This designation of the primary center direction as the province of Xiuhteuctli provides one more important piece in the Aztec mythology that defines the way in which the Aztec people viewed the world, and that is immediacy. "This centrality gave the Aztec a sense of urgency and importance; things of moment could take place in the center. This made him acutely receptive to divine commands" (p. 6). This fifth direction was both literal, as in the exact center of the crossing of the four directions, as well as metaphorical, as in the Aztec kingdom existing in the center of the world. The Aztecs organized their cities with this same divine ordering, with the center as a sacred space and temples built in each direction for the gods associated with that particular direction. With this metaphorical understanding of the Aztec kingdom existing in the central sacred space, it is clear that the mandate of the gods was inviolable here, and the gods demanded immediacy of action in this sacred fifth direction.

Before the specific gods can be considered, one more ordering of the natural world must be understood, and that is the sacred concept of time. Time is another natural phenomenon; therefore it is ruled by Xiuhteuctli, leading to his title Lord of the Year. The Aztecs had two designations for time, the natural year, or Xihuitl, and the sacred year, or Tonalpohualli. These two measures of time were different lengths, but existed simultaneously. After a cycle of 52 years, an Aztec century, both calendar counts would arrive at their last day at the same time. Within each calendar, there were months governed by gods or natural phenomena, as well as days within those months influenced by specific aspects of those gods. The combination of the day within each of the two calendars that an individual was born defined to a great extent the life and fate of the individual, as time was a divine force and not to be disputed. Another feature of this century is that it existed independently of all other centuries. When the century ended, "...it could be put down, abandoned, and a new one taken up" (p. 21). This is wholly different from both the cyclical nature of time found in Norse mythology and the linear nature of time accepted in the modern world. Time was a collection of fixed events, almost snapshots, which ended and disintegrated in order for a new event to take its place. This conception of time in many ways presages by millennia the theories of quantum theories of time or change existing as a fourth dimension which acts to dissolve and regenerate the three-dimensional world infinitely.

The pantheon of Aztec gods can be understood as a collection and procession of emanations of the source of all existence. While the Aztecs had four different creation myths that could all exist separately or in any combination with each other for the explanation of any particular feature of the universe, the primary myth is similar to many other ancient mythological structures. This is essentially creation out of chaos by the action and body of a primal pre-existent god. In the time of the Aztecs, the two brother gods Tezcatlipoca and Quetzalcoatl ruled over the earth together.

Tezcatlipoca seized control from his brother in an act that defines one of his trickster aspects—Lord of the Smoking Mirror.

 Guilhem Olivier (2008) explores the many aspects of Tezcatlipoca mythologically, psychologically, and as historical allegory in his book <u>Mockeries and Metamorphoses of an Aztec God: Tezcatlipoca, "Lord of the Smoking Mirror"</u>, and illustrates Tezcatlipoca's defeat of Quetzalcoatl as the transition point between the Toltec people and the dawn of the Aztecs. Olivier points to the story of the creation of the sun and moon in the city of Teotihuacan and Quetzalcoatl's role as "Sun of the Toltecs" (p. 162). Tezcatlipoca introduces his brother to the delights of alcohol, and in his drunken state Quetzalcoatl commits sexual transgressions against the earth itself. Tezcatlipoca carries with him a mirror of obsidian, which he urges his brother to look into; seeing himself drunken and debauched, Quetzalcoatl flees south into the desert. This aspect of Tezcatlipoca as the wielder of the mirror displays one of the key actions of the trickster, and that is revealing to man his true nature.

> We should not be surprised to find, among the deities invoked by those who confessed their sins, Tezcatlipoca next to Tlazolteotl. Penitents talked to the priest as the representative of the god: 'In front of you I undress, I stand naked. Can my actions, my acts remain secret in darkness, when in the mirror, in the light in front of you are all my acts?'...Thus it was in Tezcatlipoca's

> mirror that men's sins appeared, and thus in front of him one had to atone during the confession rituals (p. 254).

This is the truth with which Friedrich Nietzsche (2008) was grappling in <u>Beyond Good and Evil</u> when he warned us "Anyone who fights monsters should take care that he does not in the process become a monster. And if you gaze for long into an abyss, the abyss gazes back into you" (p. 68). The trickster is always waiting, just out of sight, to remind us that all of the vileness that we see before us is merely our own reflection.

With Quetzalcoatl fleeing in shame, Tezcatlipoca becomes the supreme deity, and his people, the Aztecs, arise from the traditions of the Toltecs. This myth also introduces another aspect of Tezcatlipoca as a god of ritual and sorcery. The drinking of alcohol was strictly regulated by the Toltecs, and was symbolically viewed as a poison to men. Olivier explains the transformation of this poison through divine action: "The pathogenic consequences of alcohol consumption are only transitory and, after an apparent death manifested through sleep, man is reborn when he wakes up. Drunkenness makes man similar to the deity, or rather man is possessed and the deity acts through him" (p. 144). In the religions and mythologies of many different cultures, we see that sorcery of one form or another is revered and feared. This practice of magic that is made manifest by the gods is restricted to a very small elect group of humans. At varying points throughout history, these practitioners of magic are venerated or persecuted, depending on what their art is used to achieve. Brundage (1983) discusses this aspect of Tezcatlipoca and his relation to the shamans of Mexico: "He was almost exclusively the practitioner of black magic, as one might guess from the fact that he was left-handed. If the nodal being upon which Tezcatlipoca was modeled was indeed the shaman, it was not that shaman who was accustomed to mediate between the people and the supernatural but the sorcerer of disruptive magic and furtive mind" (p. 82). It is this disruptive magic through which Tezcatlipoca, much like Prometheus and Loki, brings forth the chaos necessary to shatter the stasis that the gods of natural law seek to maintain.

In his role as the patron of sorcerers and shamans, Tezcatlipoca is a master of the art of shape shifting. This is one of the classic features of a trickster, and indeed, is necessary for a class of god that exists as an anomaly among the gods. Loki, Prometheus and Tezcatlipoca all exist as living links to the unformed anti-cosmic chaos from which creation originates, so it is only fitting that these gods are extremely comfortable employing disguises to make manifest their will. Olivier (2008) explains this shape shifting as a divine means of testing men to determine their fate. "Under the cover of night, Tezcatlipoca frightened men by taking on appearances that were as varied as they were horrible: a decapitated man with his chest split open, a funerary bundle of ashes, a giant, a groaning skull or corpse" (p. 17). The manner in which a man reacts to these manifestations will determine how Tezcatlipoca will judge the man. This is an example of the trickster being the arbiter of the fate of man, overriding the fate given him by his birth signs. It is this balance of observing the fixed nature of the universe, as dictated by the dual calendar, and the fluidity of change according to the whims of Tezcatlipoca that make up the totality of the Aztec comprehension of man's place in the world.

    These extreme tests that man is put through by Tezcatlipoca bring up another ubiquitous aspect of the trickster, and that is his position outside of the designations of good or evil. However cruel the fates of any individual may seem, they are simply individual tangles of the larger knot that the trickster is holding together. This acausal relationship between an individual's fate, his weathering of the tests of Tezcatlipoca, and the ultimate balance between order and chaos are the fundamental fluidity of the numinous at work in the realm of the mundane. In their work <u>Synchronicity: Through the Eyes of Science, Myth, and the Trickster</u>, Allan Combs and Mark Holland (2001) view this role of the trickster as the force beyond forces. "The Trickster seems not to recognize any limited aspect of reality. Like the imagination itself, he moves in a 'divine sphere of operation' which 'is no longer delineated by human wishes but rather by the totality of existence. Hence it comes about that [his] compass contains good and evil, the desirable and the disappointing, the lofty and the base'" (p. 91-92). Good and evil only exist in the minds of those in the path of the trickster, but certainly not as any real or quantifiable values in the function of operating the universe.

The trickster gods in general, and Tezcatlipoca in specific, serve an innate need of humans to grapple with their seemingly paradoxical existence. The human animal's peculiar ability to apprehend his own form and choose to direct the course of his life is in direct opposition to the natural order of his environment. There are, in the most basic terms, two possible attitudes to take towards this contradiction—to observe and define the meaning of your own human-ness, or to resist this urge to explore your meaning. The first attitude, reflection and exploration, is the province of the trickster. The second attitude, denial, is the province of the denier of man's natural (unnatural) state. Essentially, one urge is from the metaphorical serpent to eat of the tree of knowledge, and the other is a booming, noncorporeal voice saying, "don't!" This dilemma is where Tezcatlipoca defines the Aztec balancing act of destiny and random chance. In C. W. Spinks (2001) collection <u>Trickster and Ambivalence: Dance of Differentiation</u>, this balancing act is viewed through the fallible lens of the human agent in resolving this contradiction: "Aztec soothsayers, with the trickster as their patron, could appeal to human behavior as an edge to avoid failure in their readings. The trickster was born in the phenomenological basis that much in the realm of human behavior is uncertain" (p. 132). This gets much closer to the understanding of the trickster as a human invention, created in an attempt to understand the uncertainty of life on this planet.

In modern Western culture, the trickster has come to be perceived as a silly relic of our primitive past. Even the title of "trickster" seeks to dismiss the function and form of this undeniable piece of machinery in the human psyche. Carl Jung (1970) questions this minimizing attitude in <u>Four Archetypes: Mother/Rebirth/Spirit/Trickster</u>, and in fact asserts that these dismissals are validations of the trickster as an important piece of man's consciousness. Jung explains:

> Now if the myth were nothing but an historical remnant, one would have to ask why it has not long since vanished into the great rubbish-heap of the past, and why it continues to make its influence felt on the highest levels of civilization, even

> where, on account of his stupidity and grotesque scurrility, the trickster no longer plays the role of "delight-maker" (p. 142).

This speaks directly to the need for a personification of those phenomena that we cannot as of yet explain. In all likelihood, we will not, nor do I think we should, as a species, understand what makes one man paint a masterpiece, and another man murder his family. For many, gazing into that obsidian mirror of Tezcatlipoca is too unbearable. This is the eternal struggle between absolute dependency upon dogma and total responsibility and autonomy.

    The trickster embodied in Tezcatlipoca is truly the most refined and potent form of the human potential. He is bound by no natural law or contrived morality. His ability and courage to impose his will upon the world around him can be seen as either the expression of divine perfection, or, as a vile and psychopathic monster. But it is in the trickster himself that we see the truer meaning, and that is the balance at the blurred edges where these extremes push up against one another. The human sacrifices demanded by Tezcatlipoca are a spectacular example of this: one man is sacrificed to Tezcatlipoca, and goes to paradise, and a portion of his life force goes to lengthen the life of the king. There is in any one single aspect of this act, an ethical judgment that can be made, but it must be understood as a whole to understand the balance that sustained the like of the Aztecs. It was the trickster who stopped the wandering of the Chichimec people to establish the Aztec kingdom, and it was the trickster who prompted Cortes to sail across the Atlantic Ocean to subjugate and conquer the Aztec people. It is the trickster who forces us to stare into his mirror, if only to momentarily confront our most hidden selves.

Chapter 4
Set and the Egyptian Model of Balance

The ancient Egyptian world stands alone in its achievements and longevity. The Egyptian people showed a great reverence for aesthetics in their art and architecture, and our knowledge of their culture comes as much from their artistic creations as their written histories. The omnipresent features in the Egyptian arts are symmetry and balance, and this extends to all aspects of the Egyptian world. The often-repeated phrase "As above, so below" from the Emerald Tablet of Hermes Trismegistus is the Greek counterpart to the words of the Egyptian god of magic, Thoth. What is so significant about this pronouncement is that it connects the entirety of existence to the prime source: the Egyptian gods. The most fundamental application of this relationship is in the honor and worship of Set and Horus—a divine pairing that dictated the course of the entire Egyptian kingdom.

The majority of what we know about ancient Egypt comes from the Dynastic period; however, a crucial bit of information about Set and Horus comes from the foundation of the unified Egyptian kingdom. In her book <u>Images of Set: Changing Impressions of a Multi-Faceted God</u>, Joan Ann Lansberry (2013) discusses the "Scorpion King," and the imagery found in his tomb.

> King Scorpion's tomb at Abydos had a couple of ivory labels featuring Set animals. Their tails aren't the usual erect tails, and could be mistaken for Anubis, but there's another signifier which identifies

85

> them, the sedge, for while 'Horus became the lord of the papyrus country,' Set is 'the lord of the land of sedges' (p. 11).

This represents the unification of the Lower kingdom, governed by Horus, and the Upper kingdom, governed by Set. What is also significant here is that Set was the god of the desert. The desert was the wasteland that had to be endured to unite the two separated kingdoms. This desert was a vast and deadly barrier between the two kingdoms, and any king who sought to traverse this desert to bring the upper and lower lands together would surely seek the favor of Set.

    The Kings of the dynasties immediately following King Scorpion took Pharaonic names that indicated the unity of Set and Horus. In the

Second Dynasty, the Pharaoh Peribsen's successor took the name Khasekhemwy. Lansberry notes "Khasekhemwy means 'The two powers have appeared,' thereby referencing both Set and Horus" (p. 13). This idea of the two powers is a deeply held reverence for the balance and symmetry that was so predominant in Egyptian art, and by extension of life in general for the Egyptian people. To illustrate both the visual as well as philosophical reverence for symmetry, one only need look at the engraving on the side of Pharaoh Senwosret I's throne. Not only are Horus and Set visually arranged symmetrically, uniting the two lands, but also, their divine aspects are symbolically arranged to be in balance with one another.

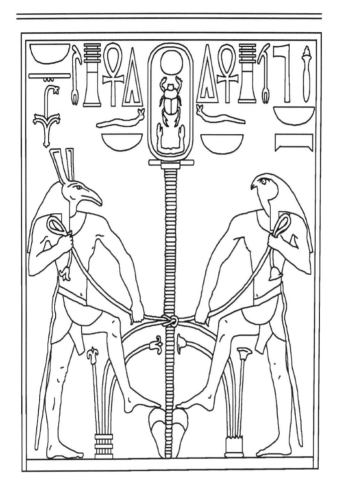

(p. 32).

Now that this relationship between Set and Horus is well established in the psyche of the pre-Dynastic and early Dynastic Egyptians, it is necessary to understand what Set and Horus represented to the Egyptians that made them the focus of the ancient Egyptian world. First, we need to once again ponder the phrase "As above, so below." The Egyptian world was not compartmentalized, as we are accustomed to in modern Western culture. The will of the gods was manifest in everything that took place in the kingdom. As opposed to the modern norm of religion, politics, commerce, and the normal profane world all being separate aspects of the individual's life, in Egypt, everything emanated from the will of the gods. Life was either lived in accordance with this divine will, or in opposition to this divine will. Serge Sauneron, (2000) in <u>The Priests of Ancient Egypt</u>, explains the relationship of the Pharaoh of the unified Egypt to the gods:

> ...the master of this new state enjoyed a higher status than had the chiefs of those small kingdoms. He was an all-powerful despot, owner of all the land and its resources, responsible for the Nile flood, for the sunrise, and for the birth of animal and plant life. Son of the gods and goddesses, he assumed responsibility for their care, and in exchange, they granted him omnipotence on earth so as to maintain the order they had defined (p. 30).

If the Pharaoh was the living link between the gods and man, then a balance between Horus and Set was necessary for the stability of life on earth.

      To understand Set's role as a trickster god, it is important to recognize the changes that Set underwent throughout the history of Ancient Egypt. The gods Horus and Set existed as regional gods of Upper and Lower Egypt before the "classical" pantheon of Egyptian gods was established. Set was the god of night, the desert, war, and "otherness." This otherness that Set represented was the separateness from nature that was manifest in man's endeavors on this earth. The desire to expand the borders and unite the two kingdoms can be seen as a manifestation of Set's proclivity for dynamic change. Horus, sometimes referred to as Horus the Elder in this context, to distinguish him from his role in later Egyptian mythology, was the god associated with the day and stability, or stasis. The Egyptian gods were originally confined to local cults, and as different regions became more powerful through the succession of the Pharaohs, the regional gods became national gods that were worshipped by the Egyptian people as a whole. Additionally, the nature of Egypt's relationship with other nations in the region began to show that perhaps the Egyptians were not the sovereign masters of the earth. A new emphasis was placed on the comfort of an afterlife to rectify any wrongs done to the citizens of Ancient Egypt. It is through this process that Set and Horus became associated with the cult of Osiris. Sauneron explains the rise of the Osirian cult:

> His success was due less to the political fortunes of his

worshippers than to the funerary nature of his functions. God of the dead in his native city of Busiris, he seems rapidly to have acquired a vast kingdom of worshippers, and in a matter of centuries, he spread throughout Egypt; around the time of Dynasty II (c. 2050 B.C.E.), he took up residence in the great city of Abydos, where, from then until the end of the history of ancient Egypt, he would figure as the great sovereign of the dead and the permanent guarantor of life in the hereafter (p. 173).

Abydos, being an early seat of power for the cult of Set from the time of the Scorpion King, naturally had to undergo a mythological revision to accommodate both Set and Osiris.

This was the beginning of the commonly known story of Set as the killer of Osiris. This narration of the death of Osiris, from David P. Silverman's (1997) <u>Ancient Egypt</u>, is the context in which most people are familiar with Set (or Seth):

> In the classical rendition, the unsuspecting Osiris was betrayed at a grand feast for the gods, where Seth offered a novel object—a coffin—as a 'party favour' to whomever it should fit. Although various gods sought to claim the prize, the coffin had been carefully made to fit Osiris alone. Once the god was securely inside, Seth and his confederates

> promptly sealed the coffin and cast it into the Nile. Osiris drowned, and death was introduced to the world (p. 134).

While this myth paints a treacherous and vile picture of Set, it does remain true to one of the most fundamental and unique aspects of the god—he is the agent of dynamic change. Set alone, through his machinations, introduced death to the world. We see this in many cultures' portrayal of the trickster; Loki brought about the death of Baldr through trickery, Tezcatlipoca tricked Quetzalcoatl into giving up his claim to rule over the Aztecs, and Prometheus betrayed Zeus to give fire to man. It is this power of the trickster that man has so long sought to reconcile: the moral judgments made on an individual act have no meaning in the workings of the universe. It is only in this change that man can experience life, and it is the trickster who seeks to force change into the static world of natural law.

The influence of Set was far from over in ancient Egypt, and in fact, one of the most prosperous periods in ancient Egypt was enjoyed under the rule of Setian Dynasties. The XIX Dynasty, commonly known as the Ramesside Period, followed an extremely tumultuous period in Ancient Egyptian history. Preceding the XIX Dynasty was the period referred to as "The Amarna Episode." During this period, Pharaoh Akhenaten, along with his Queen Nefertiti, abruptly moved the Egyptian capital to the city of Amarna and attempted to change the Egyptian State religion to a monotheistic worship of the Sun Disk, Aten. His rule saw the closing of all other temples and the removal of any inscriptions bearing the names of the other gods. After Akhenaten's brief rule, his new city of Amarna was fully destroyed, and all reference to this brief period in Egyptian history was effectively wiped out. It was after this Dynasty's final Pharaoh, Tutankhamen, that the Ramesside period began in a peculiar transitional time; and with the Ramessides came one last period of dynamic Setian change.

Sauneron (2000) discusses the dawn of the XIX Dynasty and their devotion to Set: "Born of a military family from the eastern delta, the new kings had traditionally been devoted to a deity little esteemed by the masses because of the role he had played in the death of Osiris, but who nonetheless had cult places in certain locales: the god Seth" (p. 179). Ramesses II was well aware of the danger of operating in open opposition to the Priesthood of Amun, but he also sought to fulfill his Pharaonic role as the divine representative of Set. He offered public support for the prevailing priesthood, but in a strategic move, "Ramesses sought a new sovereign pontiff for the clergy of Amun in the region of Abydos" (p. 179)! In order to faithfully fulfill his role as the ruler of the Egyptian people, but not betray his family's traditional god, he replaced the religious leader of the Priesthood of Amun with someone who he could trust in the Setian sacred city of Abydos.

The most lasting remnants of the influence of Set are in the artistic achievements of the Egyptians. The Ramesside Period saw a great flourishing of the arts, particularly with depictions of Set. What is interesting about these depictions of Set is the influence of stylistic elements from foreign countries. By the time of the XIX Dynasty, Egypt had been cross-pollinated with other cultures, from Mesopotamia, to Asia, to Greece. Lansberry (2013) describes some of these artistic representations: "Set appears (at least) three times in Seti I's tomb…For the first time we've seen so far, Set's face appears more like a donkey (aka 'ass'), than as the usual canine" (p. 89). This is a manifestation of Set's trickster nature as a shape shifter. The "As above, so below" paradigm applies here in a unique manner, as the artistic representations recognize Set's existence in other forms in different cultures, as well as the ability of Set to exist in other forms within Egypt, where there was still open hostility to his worship. The question of whether Set existed in other manifestations in these other cultures, or if his worshippers were simply attempting to relate Setian aspects to foreign gods became blurred. The reality of Set as a metaphysical presence that transcended time and culture was embraced as a reality in the Ramesside Period.

We see in this brief period of time a heightened sensitivity to the influence of Set, manifest in a deeper awareness of Set's omnipresence. The earlier ideas of the gods being regional gods were disintegrating with recognition of the qualities of Set in the gods of the foreigners. Most recognizable of the outer forms of Set was in the Mesopotamian god Baal: "On the so-called 400 year stela, Seth is not depicted in the ancient Egyptian manner with his characteristic Seth-head, but as a Baal with a human head. The features are not Egyptian but those of a foreigner, as is to be expected of gods of foreign countries" (p. 91). The recognition of the commonality of the Set/trickster archetype was present during these final Setian Dynasties. Just as we today can see the similarities between tricksters such as Loki and Prometheus, the Egyptians recognized the similarities between Set and Baal. Further, during the Ptolemaic period of Egypt, the Greeks recognized the similarities between Set and their own god Typhon. This is the unique power of the trickster—he is able to insinuate himself into the natural world, wherever seeming contradictions exist.

The gift of the trickster to man has always been that of wholeness. The gods of the natural universe can only exist in a static environment, and this static environment can't embrace the change that defines man's unique phenomenon of consciousness. The trickster, regardless of culture or form, brings self-awareness to man, and with this self-awareness, change. For it is through this consciousness that man can conceive of other forms that can be created from the universe around him. This has always been man's unbreakable link to the divine—he exists as his own creator. As above, so below. The Egyptians had the word Xeper, which means, "I have come into being." The awareness of one's own consciousness is not only evidence of man's own existence, but also evidence of man's ability to create himself according to his will. The creator and the created are inseparable.

The ways of the old kingdoms were preserved in the funerary utterances known as The Pyramid Texts, and in Samuel A. B. Mercer's

(2008) translation we see this balance of the aspect of Horus with the aspect of Set: "Between the two scepters, in this thy dignity of spirit, commanded by Anubis. If thou goest, Horus, goes; if thou speakest, Set speaks. Thou approachest the sea; thou advancest to the Thinite nome; thou passest through Abydos. A portal is open for thee in heaven, towards the horizon; the heart of the gods rejoices at thy approach" (p. 218). It is only in the balance of Horus and Set, day and night, that man approaches the divine in his completeness. The heavens embrace the individual when he acknowledges all aspects of his nature. There is no longer good or evil, there just *is*. This is both the form and the essence of the trickster—duality is simply an illusion, an illusion that allows us to see our wholeness.

References

Bobroff, G. (2014). *Crop circles, Jung, and the reemergence of the archetypal feminine.* Berkley, California: North Atlantic Books.

Brown, N. (2012.). *Song of the Vikings: Snorri and the making of Norse myths.* New York, NY: Palgrave MacMillan.

Brundage, B. (1983). *The fifth sun: Aztec gods, Aztec world*. Austin, TX: University of Texas Press.

Combs, A., & Holland, M. (2001). *Synchronicity: Through the eyes of science, myth, and the trickster* ([3rd ed.). New York, NY: Marlowe.

Dell, C. (2012). *Mythology: The complete guide to our imagined worlds*. New York: Thames & Hudson.

Hesiod, (2014). *Theogeny and Works and Days*. N/A: Stellar Editions.

Hyde, L. (2010). *Trickster makes this world: Mischief, myth, and art* (Pbk ed.). New York: Farrar, Straus and Giroux.

James, A. (2013). *The Trial of Loki: A study in Nordic Heathen morality* (Second Australian ed.). N/A: Renewal

Publications.

Jung, C. (1970). *Four archetypes; mother, rebirth, spirit, trickster.* Princeton, NJ: Princeton University Press.

Lansberry, J. (2013). *Images of set: Changing impressions of a multi -faceted god.* S.l.: Mandrake Of Oxford.

McNeely, D. (1996). *Mercury rising: Women, evil, and the trickster gods.* Woodstock, Conn.: Spring.

Mentz, G. (2014). *The Vikings - Philosophy and History - From Ragnar Lodbrok to Norse Mythology.* N/A: Metzinger Media.

Mercer, S. (2008). *The pyramid texts.* Charleston, S.C.: Forgotten Books.

Nietzsche, F. (2008). *Beyond Good and Evil.* New York, NY: Oxford University Press.

Olivier, G. (2008). *Mockeries and Metamorphoses*

of an Aztec God. Boulder, CO: Univ Pr of Colorado.

Orchard, A. (2011). *The Elder Edda: A book of Viking lore*. London: Penguin Books.

Plesiotis, N. (2014). *Greek Mythology: The complete guide to Greek Mythology, Ancient Greece, Greek Gods, Zeus, Hercules, Titans, and more!* N/A: Amazon Digital Services.

Ronnberg, A. (2010). *The book of symbols*. Köln: Taschen.

Sauneron, S., & Lorton, D. (2000). *The priests of ancient Egypt* (New ed.). Ithaca, N.Y.: Cornell University Press.

Silverman, D. (1997). *Ancient Egypt*. New York, New York: Oxford University Press.

Spinks, C. (2001). *Trickster and ambivalence: The dance of differentiation*. Madison, WI:

Atwood Pub.

Thomson, G. (1995). *Prometheus bound*. New York: Dover Publications.

Thorsson, E. (2012). *ALU, an advanced guide to operative runology: A new handbook of runes*. San Francisco, CA: Red Wheel-Weiser.

Williams, D. (2013). *The trickster brain: Neuroscience, evolution, and narrative*. Lanham, Md.: Lexington Books.

Printed in Poland
by Amazon Fulfillment
Poland Sp. z o.o., Wrocław